IMPORTANT

CREATIVE C EDUCATION

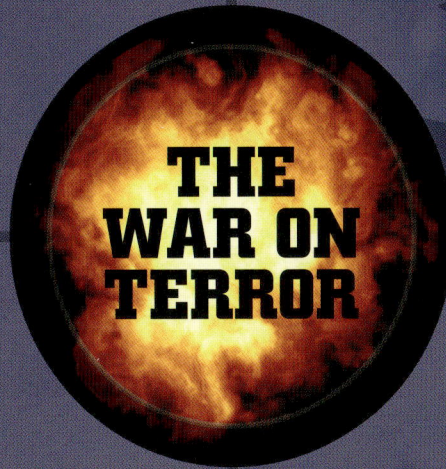

THE WAR ON TERROR

BY TERESA WIMMER

FIGURES

Published by Creative Education
P.O. Box 227, Mankato, Minnesota 56002
Creative Education is an imprint of The Creative Company
www.thecreativecompany.us

Art direction by Rita Marshall
Design and production by The Design Lab
Printed by Corporate Graphics in the United States of America

Photographs by Corbis (HO/Reuters, Rosy Rouleau/Sygma,
Sygma), Getty Images (DOD, Luke Frazza/AFP, Tim Graham, Bill
Greenblatt, Ramzi Haidar/AFP, Stephen Jaffe/AFP, David Hume
Kennerly, Saeed Khan/AFP, Wathiq Khuzaie/AFP, Saul Loeb/AFP,
A Majeed/AFP, Kimimasa Mayama/Bloomberg, Olivier Morin/AFP,
Bernd Obermann/Ovoworks/Time & Life Pictures, Scott Peterson,
Joel Saget/AFP, Fabina Sbina/Hugh Zareasky, STF/AFP, Tom
Stoddart, Mario Tama, Diana Walker/Time & Life Pictures),
iStockphotos (Lisa Gagne, Andrew Robinson)

Library of Congress Cataloging-in-Publication Data
Wimmer, Teresa.
Important figures / by Teresa Wimmer.
p. cm. — (The war on terror)
Includes bibliographical references and index.
Summary: An examination of some of the most prominent people in
the ongoing war against Islamic extremists, spotlighting such
figures as George W. Bush, Osama bin Laden, and Saddam Hussein.
ISBN 978-1-60818-100-1
1. War on Terrorism, 2001-2009—Juvenile literature. 2. Terrorism—Prevention—Juvenile literature. 3. Jihad—Juvenile literature. 4. Qaeda (Organization)—Juvenile literature. I. Title.
II. Series.

HV6431.W56635 2011
909.83'1—dc22   2010033843

CPSIA: 110310 PO1387

First Edition
9 8 7 6 5 4 3 2 1

TABLE OF CONTENTS

The September 11, 2001, attacks thrust U.S. president George W. Bush into a more active role as commander in chief of the powerful American military.

I n the late 1980s, a conflict rooted in terrorism began to rear its head on a global scale. This strife pitted Islamic fundamentalists, radical religious **militants** springing primarily from nations in the Middle East, against the countries and culture of the Western world. Spilling across parts of four decades, this conflict—which came to be known from the Western perspective as "The War on Terror"—grew from bombings and guerrilla combat into the first large-scale war of the 21st century, marked by the infamous events of September 11, 2001, and intensive military campaigns in the countries of Afghanistan and Iraq.

These conflicts in the Middle East and parts of Asia—and headline-making terror attacks in countries around the world—gave rise to individuals of various backgrounds, from both the Arab world and the West, who became prominent players on the world stage. Whether these leaders founded terrorist networks, commanded powerful military forces, or attempted to play the role of peacemaker or rebuilder, all had their supporters and detractors. From Osama bin Laden to George W. Bush to Hamid Karzai, the war pushed many individuals to the forefront of history, and the world was introduced to the differing viewpoints of leaders and common citizens on both sides.

CHAPTER ONE

THE RISE OF RADICALS

Radical fundamentalist forms of Islam, the primary root of the War on Terror, grew steadily throughout the 1960s and '70s but truly emerged as a powerful movement in 1979, when the Soviet Union invaded Afghanistan. Muslims, or followers of Islam, throughout the Middle East and south-central Asia saw the Soviets' invasion of Afghanistan as the latest in a long line of attempts at **colonialism** by non-Muslim countries. In response, many young Muslim men journeyed to Afghanistan to join the **mujahideen** and fight the Soviet army. Among these men was an Egyptian physician named Ayman al-Zawahiri.

Al-Zawahiri was born in 1951 in Cairo, Egypt, into a prominent family of doctors and politicians. His mother's father had founded King Saud University in Saudi Arabia and served as Egypt's ambassador to Pakistan, Yemen, and Saudi Arabia. In addition, his great-uncle had served as the rector, or head, of Al-Azhar University, the most prestigious Islamic school in the world. This combined exposure to politics and Islam helped shape al-Zawahiri's **ideology** as a child.

As a teenager, al-Zawahiri adopted the belief that Egypt needed to return to its Islamic roots and organized a secretive movement to overthrow the Egyptian government, which had become more **secular** under president

Many Afghanis who were no older than boys took up arms as members of the mujahideen during the Soviet War in Afghanistan.

Gamal Abdel Nasser, and create an Islamic state. After graduating from medical school in 1974, al-Zawahiri served for three years as a surgeon in the Egyptian army and, in 1980, went to Pakistan to help the tens of thousands of Afghan refugees who were fleeing the Soviet occupation of their homeland. In 1981, al-Zawahiri was imprisoned for being part of the group accused of assassinating Egyptian president Anwar al-Sadat, who had signed a peace agreement with Israel. Years later,

al-Zawahiri would remark, "With the killing of Anwar al-Sadat, the issue of **jihad** … exploded and became a daily practice." Although al-Zawahiri did not know him well at the time, Osama bin Laden—who would later become al-Zawahiri's ideological and terrorist partner—was also inspired to come to the aid of the mujahideen.

Osama bin Laden was born in 1957 in Saudi Arabia, where his father had started a prosperous construction business. Through its projects in Saudi Arabia, the bin Laden family became close to the Saudi king and therefore had privileged access to

Egyptian president Anwar al-Sadat

Oil has made Saudi Arabia a wealthy country, as it holds about one-fifth of the world's known supply.

MAKING A FORTUNE

After oil was discovered in Saudi Arabia in the late 1930s, Osama bin Laden's father, Mohammed bin Laden, moved there from Yemen to make his fortune in the construction business. Although Mohammed was illiterate when he arrived, he proved to have a genius for business and constructed roads, mosques, hotels, and Saudi family palaces throughout the vast Saudi Arabian countryside. Mohammed died in a plane crash in 1967, leaving his $11-billion fortune to his estimated 56 children, including 10-year-old Osama.

TACTICAL LEADER

Mohamed Atta, an Egyptian architect, was recruited by Osama bin Laden in 1999 to be the tactical leader of al Qaeda's 2001 attacks on America. Upon his arrival in Kandahar, Afghanistan, he immediately impressed bin Laden as being ruthless and eager to achieve **martyrdom**. Atta arrived in the U.S. in June 2000 to take flight lessons in Venice, Florida. On 9/11, Atta was the hijacker-pilot who crashed American Airlines Flight 11 into the north tower of the World Trade Center, killing all 92 people aboard and causing the skyscraper to collapse.

Osama bin Laden

the inner circles of politics in Saudi Arabia, one of the richest and most powerful countries in the Middle East. The **Wahhabi** form of Islam had for many years provided the religious and ideological foundation of Saudi Arabia, and it would have a huge impact on forming Osama bin Laden's radical beliefs.

As a child, bin Laden often visited Syria with his mother, who had grown up there. During that time, Syria was at war with Israel, and this early exposure also played a role in shaping bin Laden's anti-Western and anti-Israeli views. Bin Laden attended business management school at King Abdulaziz University in Jeddah, Saudi Arabia. While there, he took courses on Islam and was recruited to join the **Muslim Brotherhood**. Leaving college short of graduation, he traveled throughout the Saudi kingdom overseeing his late father's construction projects. However, he did not feel he had yet found his true purpose in life.

After the Soviets invaded Afghanistan, bin Laden traveled there to join the jihad and became a major financier of the mujahideen, funding any Arab who wanted to travel to Afghanistan to join the fight. Increasing numbers of young Arabs heeded his call. In the late 1980s, he began calling his group al Qaeda, Arabic for "the base." Wealthy, charismatic, and devout, bin Laden was uniquely qualified to emerge as a Muslim leader, and he quickly became a celebrity and hero to many in the Middle East.

At first, the mujahideen seemed to be at an extreme disadvantage in battling the huge, well-equipped Soviet army, and its defeat seemed imminent. However, backed by funding from the United States (at that time an enemy of the Soviets), Pakistan, and six other countries, the mujahideen drove the Soviet army out of Afghanistan in February 1989. Although it was a great victory for Afghans and the mujahideen, the decade-long war had left Afghanistan in shambles. The mujahideen were not equipped to set up a government, and civil war soon broke out. Out of this chaos rose the Taliban and its leader, Mullah Mohammed Omar.

The Taliban (whose name means "seekers of knowledge") formed in Kandahar, Afghanistan, in 1994 as a small group that followed the teachings of Omar, an Islamic cleric who had lost one eye during the Soviet conflict. Omar was likely born in 1959 in Oruzgan Province, one of the poorest regions of Afghanistan. He was educated mainly in the **madrasas**, where he was introduced to Islamic ideology. Omar wanted to purge Afghanistan of its warring parties and install a pure, Islamic government that would restore law and order. At first, Afghans welcomed Omar's Taliban for its ability to restore order to society and incorporate Islamic laws and values back into everyday life. But as the Taliban quickly took over three of Afghanistan's five biggest cities by 1996, including the capital of Kabul, its extremist and often brutal religious and political agenda became apparent. This new ruling party would soon become even stronger by partnering with al Qaeda.

Afghan refugees in Pakistan protest in 2000 against the widespread violence caused by the Taliban and its fundamentalist laws.

In 1990, when the Iraqi army invaded Kuwait, neighboring Saudi Arabia felt threatened. Bin Laden offered to assist his homeland by sending fighters, but Prince Sultan al Saud had already accepted an offer by the U.S. to send 250,000 soldiers to protect Saudi Arabia. In late 1994, bin Laden criticized Saudi leaders for inviting Americans into holy Muslim cities and called for jihad to remove the "corrupt" Saudi government. In response, the Saudis revoked bin Laden's citizenship. He spent time in Sudan and then, in May 1996, fled to Afghanistan, where he was welcomed by the Taliban.

In 1997, bin Laden joined forces with al-Zawahiri, who became the spokesman for al Qaeda because of his education and good command of the English language. In February 1998, bin Laden, al-Zawahiri, and three other prominent jihadists publicly declared war on America, citing three main grievances: U.S. occupation of Islam's holy land; the suffering of Iraqis as a result of sanctions, or punishments, imposed by the **United Nations (UN)** beginning in 1991; and the 1948 founding of Israel and its occupation of the holy city of Jerusalem. Radical Islam had found its leaders.

U.S. troops, shown here arriving in Saudi Arabia, made up almost 75 percent of the coalition force opposing Iraq during the Persian Gulf War.

THE BIRTH OF ISRAEL

After World War II (1939–1945), the victorious Allies wanted to provide a way for European Jews—who had been persecuted by Nazi Germany during the war—to return to their historical homeland. In 1948, the UN carved out a portion of Palestine and created the nation of Israel. Almost immediately, Palestinians (who were mainly Arab Muslims) fought to regain their land and remove Israeli Jews from the holy city of Jerusalem. Soon, other Arabs in the Middle East took up arms to support the Palestinian cause, leading to a bloody Arab-Israeli conflict that continues today.

CHAPTER TWO

FRIENDS AND ENEMIES

In 1998—after al Qaeda had used bomb-laden trucks to attack American embassies in Kenya and Tanzania, resulting in nearly 300 deaths—bin Laden began plotting with a Pakistani terrorist named Khalid Sheikh Mohammed to use airplanes to attack the U.S. mainland. Mohammed masterminded the attacks, and bin Laden recruited the men who would be involved from the large pool of al Qaeda volunteers. On the morning of September 11, 2001, 19 al Qaeda terrorists hijacked 4 airliners bound from the East Coast to the West Coast; two crashed into the "Twin Towers" of New York's World Trade Center, one into the **Pentagon** in Washington, D.C., and one into

a field in Pennsylvania. Nearly 3,000 people died, making it the deadliest attack ever to occur on American soil.

Bin Laden and al-Zawahiri soon claimed responsibility for the "9/11" attacks and stated publicly that their objective was to incite the U.S. and its allies to retaliate by invading Afghanistan and entering into a long, bloody war. As bin Laden later stated in a 2004 message, "We bled Russia for 10 years, until it ... was forced to withdraw in defeat, thanks be to God. So we are continuing this policy in bleeding America." Al Qaeda hoped the U.S. would launch a massive counterattack, be defeated by Afghanistan's guerrilla warriors, and be

Al Qaeda terrorists' willingness to die allowed them to turn airliners into missiles, which they used to destroy the World Trade Center towers.

INSPIRATION FOR 9/11

Khalid Sheikh Mohammed modeled the 9/11 attacks on a December 1994 attack in Algiers, Algeria, in which four Algerian terrorists, dressed as policemen, took control of Air France Flight 8969 as it prepared for takeoff to Paris. After French authorities learned that the terrorists planned to crash the plane into the Eiffel Tower, they persuaded them to land in Marseilles to refuel. French commandos then stormed the plane, killing the terrorists. Of the 232 total passengers and crew, 229 were saved, but the event illustrated the growing strength of the Islamic jihadist movement.

forced out of the Arab Muslim world. However, instead of retaliating with a large-scale attack, U.S. president George W. Bush set a course of using **diplomacy** and calculated force to bring al Qaeda—and its Taliban supporters—to justice.

Bush was born in 1946 in New Haven, Connecticut. He came from a family of politicians. His father, George H. W. Bush, had served as U.S. president from 1989 to 1993, and his grandfather, Prescott Bush, had been a U.S. senator. After

President George W. Bush

graduating from Yale University in 1968, Bush joined the Texas Air National Guard, becoming a certified fighter pilot in 1970. Granted an early discharge to enroll in Harvard Business School, he received a master's degree in business in 1975 and then returned to Texas, where he started his own oil and gas company, Arbusto Energy, and married schoolteacher Laura Welch in 1977.

As a young man, Bush enjoyed parties and drank excessively; however, at the age of 40, he found Christianity and became a devoted prayer group member. He would later cite this newfound faith, and the influence of his wife, as the elements that made him stop drinking and change the course of his life. In 1994, Bush was elected governor of Texas, making history by becoming the first child of a former U.S. president to serve as state governor. His natural charisma and straight-talking manner helped earn him reelection in 1998 by a wide margin. Soon after, he announced his candidacy for president. In 2000, Bush, a Republican, defeated Democratic candidate Al Gore by one of the narrowest margins in the history of U.S. presidential elections.

Just eight months after taking office, Bush was forced to respond to the 9/11 attacks, and the War on Terror would come to define his presidency. His conservative Christian viewpoint would continue to play an important role in his life and decisions, earning him both devoted admirers and skeptical critics at home and abroad, and creating tension between him and many increasingly secular European leaders. "I never want to impose my religion on anybody else," Bush said in a 2004 presidential debate. "But when I make decisions, I stand on principle."

SLIM VICTORY

George W. Bush was elected president in 2000 by one of the slimmest margins in U.S. history. When the election returns came in, Bush had won 29 states, while Democratic candidate Al Gore had won 21. However, Bush lost the popular vote by 543,895 votes. Because the outcome in Florida was extremely close, officials spent five weeks recounting the votes, and the U.S. Supreme Court weighed in on the process. In the end, Bush won Florida by 537 votes and thus became the nation's 43rd president.

After 9/11, Bush asked the Taliban to surrender bin Laden. When it refused, the U.S. and a **coalition** of allies launched Operation Enduring Freedom, a military campaign intended to topple the Taliban and capture or kill al Qaeda leaders. The UN sanctioned this action, and many European countries joined the effort. At first, the coalition forces focused heavily on air attacks, bombing the compounds and mountain hideouts of al Qaeda and the Taliban. After several weeks of limited success, they began to work closely on the ground with the Northern Alliance, which was still recovering from the death of its commander, Ahmad Shah Massoud.

Born in 1953 in Bazarak, Afghanistan, Massoud was the son of a police commander. A gifted student, he spoke many languages, including Persian, Arabic, French, and English. While studying engineering at Kabul University, Massoud became involved with the Organization of Muslim Youth, a group that opposed the Soviets' influence in Afghanistan. During the Soviet War in Afghanistan, Massoud organized a guerrilla force that helped to drive the Soviets from the country, and the Afghan people nicknamed him the "Lion

An Afghan boy at the grave of Ahmad Shah Massoud; a sign near Massoud's mountaintop resting place reads "The Chief of the Martyrs Hill."

ATTACK ON MASSOUD

On September 9, 2001, two days before the 9/11 attacks, Osama bin Laden repaid Taliban leader Mullah Mohammed Omar for hosting al Qaeda by organizing a plot to kill Ahmad Shah Massoud, the leader of the Northern Alliance and Omar's chief enemy. Two al Qaeda members, posing as journalists, entered Massoud's office to interview him, and explosives hidden inside their camera then detonated. The al Qaeda cameraman was killed instantly, and Massoud died within a few minutes.

of Panjshir" for his strength and intelligence in battle. In July 1983, he created a military council that coordinated the actions of 130 tribal chiefs and warlords from 7 provinces in northern Afghanistan. In the 1990s, this group, which became known as the Northern Alliance, fought against the Taliban's increasing control over the country. Massoud was assassinated by al Qaeda two days before the 9/11 attacks.

Although the Northern Alliance proved to be a valuable partner to the coalition, Bush knew that Pakistan's support would also be vital in defeating the Taliban and al Qaeda in Afghanistan. Taking a firm stance, he told Pakistan's president, General Pervez Musharraf, that Pakistan could either help the U.S. or be seen as an enemy.

Almost immediately, Musharraf deserted the Taliban—which had received support from Pakistan since the Soviet War in Afghanistan—and began cooperating with the coalition.

The son of a diplomat and a UN worker, Musharraf was born in 1943 in Delhi, India, and raised in Pakistan and Turkey. In 1961, Musharraf enrolled in the Pakistan Military Academy, and after completing his military education, he fought in the 1965 and 1971 Indo-Pakistani wars, earning promotion to captain. Self-confident and persevering, he continued to rise through the ranks and was eventually appointed chief of army staff in 1998. In 1999, Musharraf led a military coup to seize control of the Pakistani government, and he appointed himself president in 2001.

In a January 2002 speech, Pakastani president Pervez Musharraf publicly condemned terrorism and pledged to combat jihadist organizations.

RIGHT-HAND MAN

When George W. Bush was elected U.S. president in 2000, vice president Dick Cheney became his closest adviser. Highly regarded among fellow Republicans, Cheney promoted an expansion of presidential powers after 9/11, including the president's right to detain suspected terrorists without charging them with a specific crime. In 2003, he became one of the Bush administration's biggest advocates for the invasion of Iraq. Although he had a gruff personal manner and preferred to stay behind the scenes, Cheney was known for his intelligence and clout, earning a reputation as one of the most influential vice presidents in U.S. history.

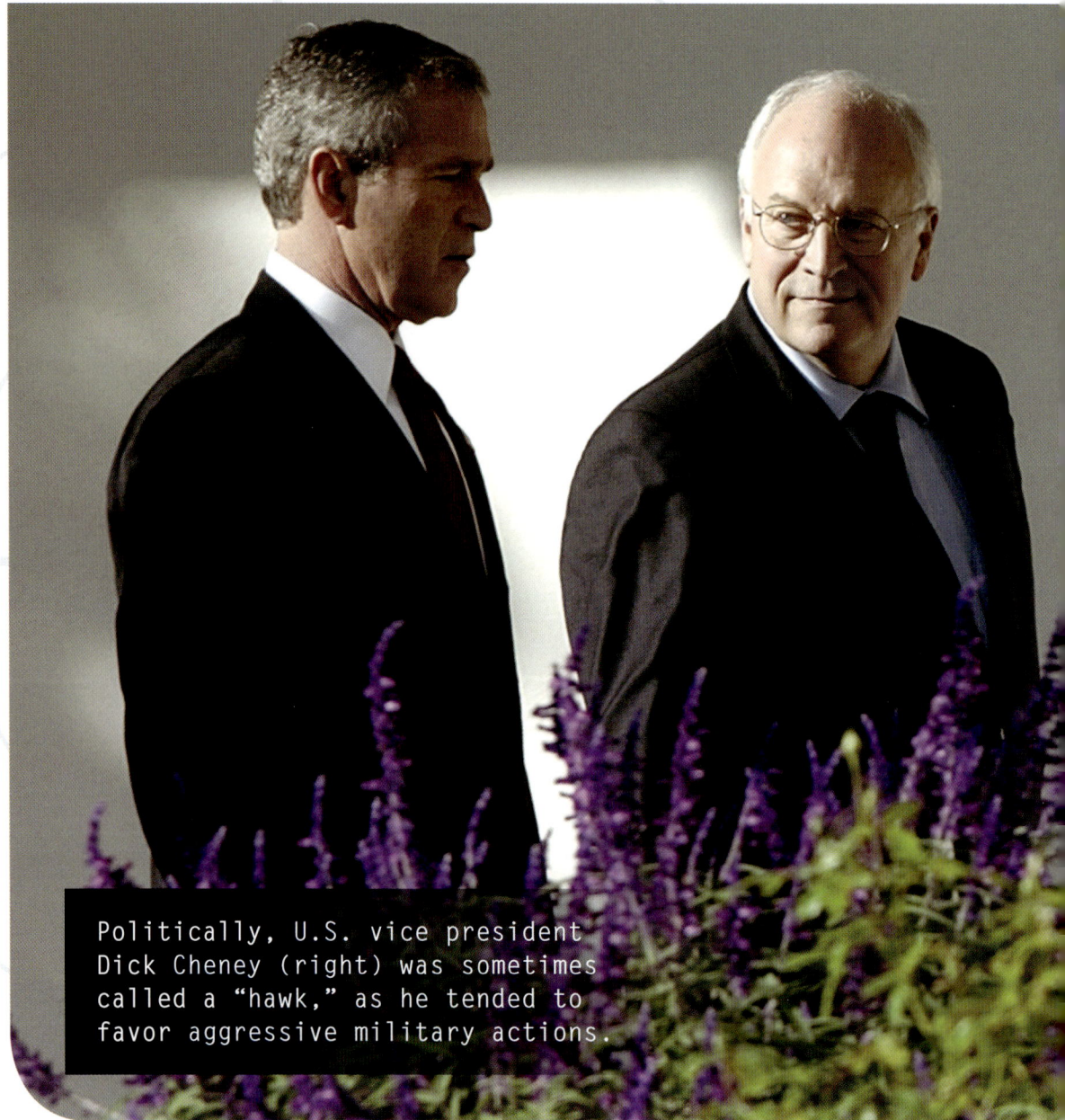

Politically, U.S. vice president Dick Cheney (right) was sometimes called a "hawk," as he tended to favor aggressive military actions.

With Pakistan's economy in a weak position, and reluctant to be at odds with America, Musharraf agreed to give the U.S. access to its airbases after 9/11 in order to launch attacks on the Taliban. His cooperation with America angered Islamic fundamentalists in Pakistan and Afghanistan, and from 2001 to 2008, Musharraf would be the target of several unsuccessful assassination attempts.

Without Pakistan's support, the Taliban was greatly weakened. Within weeks, the coalition forces—composed mainly of troops from the U.S., Great Britain, Australia, Poland, Denmark, and Spain—and the Northern Alliance had defeated the Taliban and trapped al Qaeda leaders along the border between Pakistan and Afghanistan. By the end of 2001, Omar's Taliban had been removed from power, and al Qaeda had been dealt a serious blow. However, by March 2002, as the coalition forces appeared close to capturing bin Laden and other terrorist leaders, Bush and his administration began rerouting troops toward Iraq in preparation for a new invasion.

CHAPTER THREE

A SECOND INVASION

Bush and members of his administration considered Iraqi president Saddam Hussein to be one of the greatest threats in the Middle East. Specifically, they worried that he possessed **weapons of mass destruction (WMD)** and might sell them to terrorist organizations such as al Qaeda. Born in 1937 near Tikrit, Iraq, Hussein grew up very poor. He attended Cairo Law School in 1962 and Baghdad Law College in 1963 and quickly became a leader within the Baath Party (an Arab political party prominent in Iraq at that time). By 1968, Hussein had become second-in-command under president Ahmad Hasan al-Bakr, and when al-Bakr resigned in 1979, Hussein assumed total control of the government. As Iraq's president, he quickly gained a reputation as a ruthless dictator, employing secret police to suppress Iraqis opposing his rule and systematically using rape, torture, and executions against anyone he perceived as a threat.

After Iraq was defeated in the Persian Gulf War of 1991, Hussein was ordered by the UN to dismantle all WMD and long-range missiles. However, he often refused to allow UN weapons inspectors into the country to verify his cooperation, and the U.S. and some of its allies believed he remained in possession of WMD. After the 9/11 attacks, Bush, vice president Dick Cheney, and U.S. secretary of

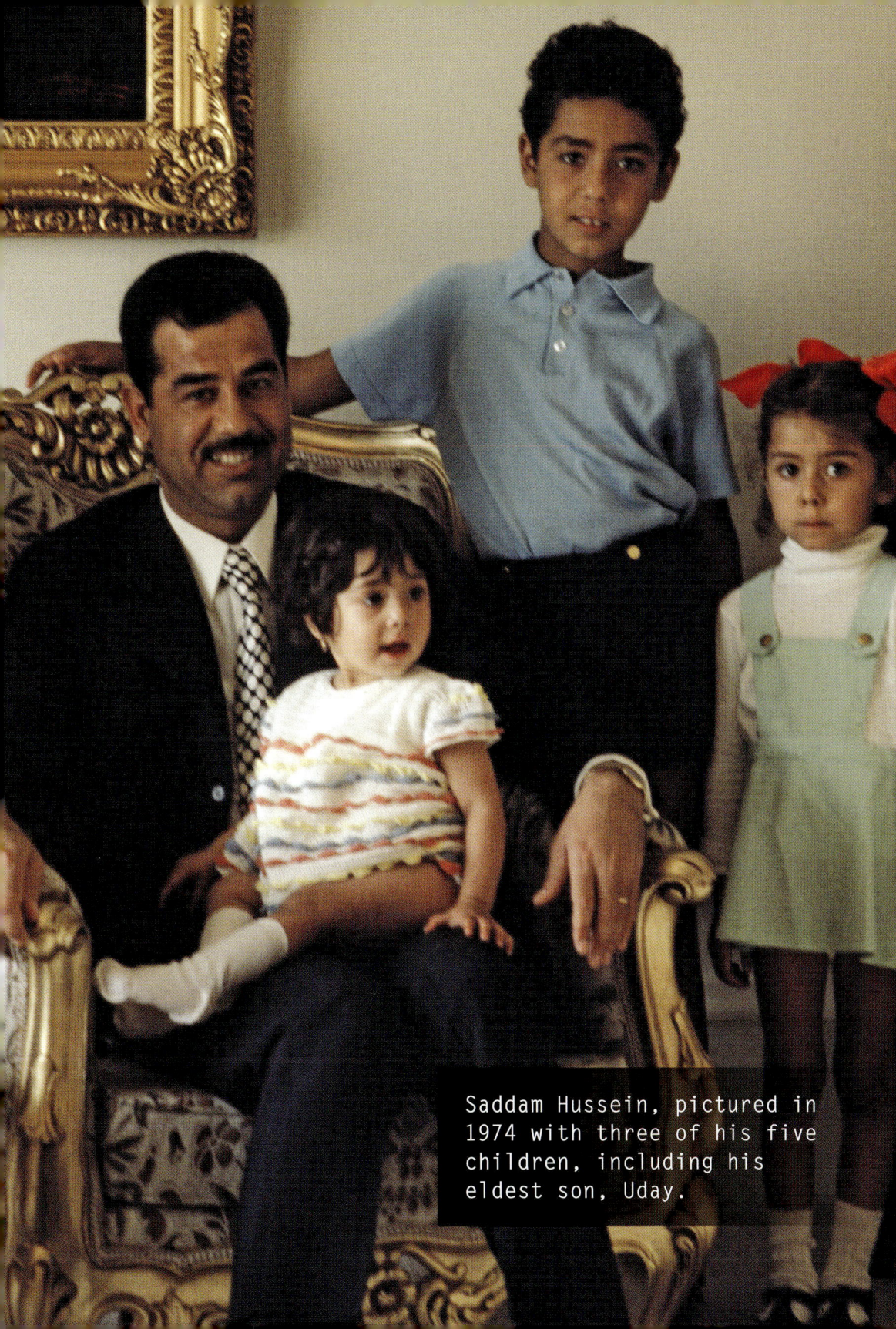

Saddam Hussein, pictured in 1974 with three of his five children, including his eldest son, Uday.

ALL IN THE FAMILY

Saddam Hussein's family gained an increasingly ruthless reputation throughout the 1990s. As the head of Iraq's national sports organization, Hussein's eldest son, Uday, reportedly tortured members of the national soccer team if they did not play well. In 1995, two of Hussein's daughters and their husbands fled to Jordan and then spoke in favor of Hussein's removal from power. In February 1996, they were persuaded to return to Iraq, where Hussein quickly had his sons-in-law murdered. In July 2003, Uday and his brother Qusay were killed by U.S. soldiers.

GULF WAR SANCTIONS

In 1991, at the end of the Persian Gulf War, Iraq was forced to leave Kuwait—the neighboring country it had invaded the previous year—and to dismantle all WMD. However, when Iraqi president Saddam Hussein refused to allow UN weapons inspectors to verify that he had complied, the UN imposed sanctions on Iraq, which restricted Iraq's import of food, supplies, and medical care and led to high rates of illness. This increased the suffering of many Iraqis, who also remained oppressed by Hussein's dictatorship.

One of the most iconic images of the Iraq War was the felling of a Saddam Hussein statue when coalition forces reached Baghdad in April 2003.

defense Donald Rumsfeld believed there was a link between Hussein and bin Laden, and they were determined to remove the threat. On March 20, 2003, the U.S. and a coalition of allies launched Operation Iraqi Freedom to remove Hussein from power.

The son of a real estate salesman, Donald Rumsfeld was born in 1932 in Chicago, Illinois. He wrestled competitively in high school and at Princeton University, where he graduated in 1954 with a degree in political science. After moving to Washington, D.C., in 1957, Rumsfeld started out as a congressional assistant but quickly moved up the political ladder, winning election to the House of Representatives in 1962. In 1969, Rumsfeld gave up his position to serve on president Richard Nixon's cabinet, and in the mid-1970s, he served for two years as U.S. ambassador to the **North Atlantic Treaty Organization (NATO)** before retiring to private business.

In 2001, Rumsfeld was appointed by Bush as the 21st U.S. secretary of defense, and he soon began to modernize the U.S. military so that it relied more upon high-tech weapons and air power and less upon large numbers of ground troops. Rumsfeld was known for his blunt, authoritative manner of speaking, which rubbed some people—including other U.S. government officials and European leaders—the wrong way. As Rumsfeld and the Bush administration sought foreign support before the invasion of Iraq, they found their most resolute ally in Britain and its prime minister, Tony Blair.

Donald Rumsfeld held many government positions throughout his long political career. He served as secretary of defense under president Gerald Ford from 1975 to 1977 and again under president George W. Bush from 2001 to 2006, making him both the youngest and oldest person to hold that post. In 1983 and 1984, Rumsfeld served as president Ronald Reagan's special envoy to the Middle East and played an important role in funneling American military aid to Saddam Hussein, who was fighting Iran (a U.S. enemy at the time) in the Iran-Iraq War.

As special envoy to the Middle East in the 1980s, Donald Rumsfeld (right) had a cordial relationship with Saddam Hussein, whom he would later help remove from power.

Like Bush, and unlike many of his European counterparts, Blair was a practicing Christian who held his faith close. Born in 1953 in Edinburgh, Scotland, Blair grew up in a middle-class family, becoming a mischievous but popular student. While studying law at St. John's College, Oxford, he developed a deep concern for religious faith and liberal politics. Blair joined the Labour Party soon after graduating in 1975 and began running for office in the early 1980s. He quickly

British prime minister Tony Blair

made a name for himself. On May 2, 1997, the 43-year-old Blair became Britain's youngest prime minister in nearly 200 years.

Blair was a valuable U.S. partner from the start, and after 9/11, he promised unconditional support to the Bush administration in its war in Afghanistan. In 2003, Britain became America's primary ally in its invasion of Iraq when Blair promised 45,000 troops to assist the 248,000 U.S. troops. However, Blair's support for the Bush administration separated him from much of the British population and members of his own party, many of whom

DISTINGUISHED PEACEMAKER

In January 2009, president George W. Bush awarded British prime minister Tony Blair the Presidential Medal of Freedom for his support during the War on Terror and his role in achieving peace in Northern Ireland (which had long seen violence between Protestants and Catholics). That same year, Blair was awarded the Dan David Prize by Tel Aviv University in Israel for his leadership and determination in helping to forge lasting solutions to areas in conflict.

opposed the Iraq invasion. Bush and Blair were prepared to take risks to end Hussein's reign of power, but many other global leaders, such as French president Jacques Chirac and Russian president Vladimir Putin, were not. "The threat from Saddam Hussein and weapons of mass destruction—chemical, biological, potentially nuclear weapons capability—that threat is real," Blair stated in a 2003 speech. However, what Bush and Blair thought would be a relatively quick victory in Iraq would prove to be anything but.

Although coalition forces captured the Iraqi capital of Baghdad after just 21 days of fighting, and although Bush declared on May 1, 2003, that major combat operations in Iraq had ended, Iraqi **insurgents** then began launching attacks against coalition troops. By the summer of 2004, more than 1,000 coalition troops, 130 foreign workers, and thousands of Iraqi civilians had been killed. American **intelligence** leaders and General Tommy Franks, the U.S. commander in Iraq, publicly acknowledged that they had not anticipated that armed insurgent groups could attack as quickly and violently as they did. The coalition also did not foresee the mayhem that Abu Musab al-Zarqawi, the leader of al Qaeda in Iraq, would cause.

Born in Zarqa, Jordan, in 1966, al-Zarqawi grew up near a large Palestinian refugee camp, which became a breeding ground for anti-Israeli politics. When al-Zarqawi was 17, he dropped out of school, turned to crime, and was arrested for drug possession and assault. In prison, he found Islam and became a strong believer in Wahhabi and extremist ideals. In 1999, after spending more time in prison for plotting an

Abu Musab al-Zarqawi

attack against the king of Jordan, al-Zarqawi came into contact with bin Laden and other al Qaeda leaders. In early 2000, bin Laden and al-Zawahiri agreed to allow al-Zarqawi to operate closely with al Qaeda from an independent camp in Iraq.

After the U.S.-led invasion of Iraq in 2003, al-Zarqawi and al Qaeda put their latest plan into action. Hoping to isolate American forces and destabilize Iraq, al-Zarqawi directed some of the country's most frequent and violent insurgent attacks, many in the form of car bombings or hidden explosives. He took a very active

THE PRICE OF PEACE

In September 1993, the Oslo Accords—an agreement by which Israel gave some of its land back to Palestine in exchange for the right to peacefully co-exist—were signed by Palestinian chairman Yasser Arafat and Israeli prime minister Yitzhak Rabin. In response, Osama bin Laden called for jihad against the West, Jews, and "corrupt" Arab governments in order to recover Islamic lands. He also wrote a letter to Saudi Arabia, denouncing his home country for supporting the Accords. This letter marked bin Laden's shift from critic to terrorist.

The extensive mountains of Afghanistan and neighboring Pakistan provided remote hideouts for Osama bin Laden and other al Qaeda leaders.

role in this terrorism, even allegedly beheading Western hostages—such as American construction worker Nick Berg—and filming his acts for **propaganda** purposes. His extreme views and violent attacks on **Shiites** and other Iraqi civilians drew condemnation from people around the world and earned him the nickname "The Stranger," even among his fellow jihadists. After months of hunting, American forces finally located and killed al-Zarqawi with an air strike on June 7, 2006.

Yet even after al-Zarqawi's death, the War on Terror was far from over. By 2006, the Taliban had regrouped in Afghanistan and was launching new insurgent attacks there. Although the U.S. captured Mohammed in March 2003, other al Qaeda leaders remained free in the mountains of Afghanistan and Pakistan, where they plotted new attacks. Even though Musharraf had pledged that Pakistan would support the coalition's campaign in Afghanistan and work to stop terrorists from crossing the Pakistan-Afghanistan border, many U.S. officials began to question Pakistan's commitment to the cause.

CHAPTER FOUR

NEW LEADERS, NEW CHANGE

As 2008 began, it appeared that the tide was turning in the Iraq War. Thanks to a surge of 20,000 new U.S. troops sent to the country in 2007 and to a newfound cooperation between **Sunni** tribal leaders and coalition forces, insurgent violence had fallen sharply. However, Iraqi prime minister Nouri al-Maliki, who was named to the post in April 2006, still faced many challenges in establishing order in Iraq and in proving himself capable of leading the Iraqi people.

Al-Maliki was born in 1950 near Al-Hillah, Iraq, and earned a master's degree in Arabic literature from Baghdad University. In the late 1960s, he joined the Islamic Dawa Party, an underground political movement that worked to oppose the political party of Saddam Hussein. In 1979, al-Maliki fled Iraq after learning that Hussein was planning to kill him and other Dawa Party members for their resistance activities. He moved to Syria, where he directed guerrilla forces against Hussein's regime until the 2003 invasion of Iraq.

As prime minister, al-Maliki worked to unify Iraq's different religious and political groups. He also played a key role in drafting

Iraqi prime minister Nouri al-Maliki

the Status of Forces agreement with the U.S., an arrangement mandating that American forces be out of Iraqi cities by June 2009 (U.S. troops remained in the country but moved to military bases after that date). As a result of his successful dealings with the U.S., al-Maliki's reputation soared among the Iraqi people.

Meanwhile, coalition attempts at handing over authority to a new government in Afghanistan had more mixed results. In 2004, Afghanistan's first free election was held.

Afghan president Hamid Karzai

Despite Taliban threats and attacks, voters turned out in high numbers and elected Hamid Karzai president. Born into a distinguished family (his father was deputy speaker of the Afghan parliament) in 1957 in Karz, Afghanistan, Karzai was a good student and learned to speak multiple languages, including Persian, Hindi, French, and English. During the Soviet War in Afghanistan, he worked as a fundraiser for the mujahideen, and in 1994, Karzai began working to oppose the Taliban, aligning himself closely with Massoud and the Northern Alliance in early 2001.

Even after Karzai became president, his government had limited authority over much of rural Afghanistan, which was controlled mainly by local warlords. Karzai was successful in authorizing the rebuilding of many schools and bridges and helping to draw up a new national constitution. The country's economy also grew as people began reinvesting money in Afghan industries, and millions of refugees returned. However, the Afghan people's confidence in Karzai's government began to wane by 2006, as allegations spread that government officials and police officers were closely linked with opium drug lords. Karzai, however, kept up his efforts to end the war and restore Afghanistan's independence. In a statement made at a national peace conference in June 2010, he told Taliban militants that continued fighting would only prevent the withdrawal of international forces from Afghanistan. "Make peace with me, and there will be no need for foreigners here," Karzai said.

The ongoing instability and violence made coalition nations reluctant to withdraw troops from Afghanistan. In 2006, International Security Assistance Force (ISAF) troops, under the direction of

THE KARZAI LEGACY

Hamid Karzai—whose family were members of the Pashtun people (the largest ethnic group in Afghanistan)—came from a long line of respected Afghan leaders. Karzai's grandfather was president of the Afghan national council under king Mohammed Zahir Shah (who ruled from 1933 to 1973), and his father served in the king's parliament. Karzai had seven siblings—six brothers and one sister—five of whom lived in the U.S., where they ran a chain of Afghan restaurants called Helmand.

NEW LEADERS, NEW CHANGE

NATO, began taking over for U.S. troops in southern Afghanistan but had difficulty maintaining peace in cities from which the Taliban had been previously removed. In 2009, U.S. Army General Stanley A. McChrystal, who was then commander of all coalition forces in Afghanistan, told newly elected U.S. president Barack Obama that unless 40,000 more troops were deployed to Afghanistan, the military campaign would be headed for failure.

Many Americans—as well as many Europeans and Arabs—had grown opposed to the Bush administration's aggressive foreign policies and military strategies in Iraq and Afghanistan and cheered Obama's election in 2008. Obama was born in 1961 in Honolulu, Hawaii, to an American mother and Kenyan father. His father abandoned the family when Barack was a young child, and Obama grew up largely in the care of his grandparents. After graduating from Columbia University in 1983, Obama worked as a community organizer for low-income families in Chicago. Obama's advocacy work led him to run for, and win, a seat in the Illinois Senate in 1996.

Following the 9/11 attacks, Obama was an early opponent of President Bush's Iraq strategy, speaking out against a resolution authorizing the use of force against Iraq. Encouraged by his resounding election to the U.S. Senate in 2004, he decided to run for president in 2008. In November 2008, Obama became the first African American to be elected U.S. president, and

U.S. president Barack Obama accepts the Nobel Peace Prize in December 2009.

A CONTROVERSIAL PRIZE

In October 2009, U.S. president Barack Obama was named the winner of the Nobel Peace Prize. While the award drew praise from much of the world, many people saw the honor as premature, noting that Obama—having been president a mere nine months—had not yet accomplished much on the world stage. The Nobel Committee hailed Obama for his willingness to reach out to the Islamic world, his commitment to stopping the spread of nuclear weapons, and his stated goal of bringing Israelis and Palestinians into serious negotiations for peace.

MAHMOUD AHMADINEJAD

Elected president of Iran in 2005, Mahmoud Ahmadinejad quickly became a controversial figure. The religiously conservative Ahmadinejad was known to imprison anyone he perceived as threatening his rule, and in the summer of 2009, he admitted to stockpiling uranium (the main element used in making nuclear weapons), even though it was against **nuclear nonproliferation** policy. In response, the UN imposed sanctions on Iran in 2010, which barred all countries from allowing Iran to invest in their nuclear technology. Ahmadinejad, however, vowed that Iran would continue enriching uranium, dismissing the sanctions as "annoying flies."

Iranian president Mahmoud Ahmadinejad, accompanied by scientists, visits the Natanz nuclear enrichment facility in central Iran.

he immediately reached out to improve relations with world leaders. "The defeat of international terrorism ... will require the cooperation of many nations," he said. "Our success in doing so is enhanced by engaging our allies." In 2009, Obama ordered an additional 30,000 troops to be deployed to Afghanistan. In keeping with his campaign vow to change the course of the War on Terror, he then withdrew 20,000 combat troops from Iraq in the summer of 2010, setting a date of December 2011 for complete withdrawal, and refocused U.S. military and intelligence efforts on finding bin Laden and other top al Qaeda leaders.

By late 2009, many Taliban insurgents had been driven by the coalition's pursuit to remote areas of northwest Afghanistan and Pakistan, but their violent resistance to the coalition continued. With the help of Pakistani Taliban leader Hakimullah Mehsud, the Taliban ratcheted up its violence, frequently planting roadside bombs inside Pakistan to attack NATO vehicles as they brought aid

Hakimullah Mehsud

coalition forces and Afghan citizens. The U.S. struck a huge blow against al Qaeda on May 2, 2011, when it finally located bin Laden hiding out in a compound in northern Pakistan and killed him during a nighttime raid. The news made global headlines and represented a major victory for the coalition, but it did not mean an end to the conflict. Although U.S. counterterrorism officials estimated that al Qaeda members in Afghanistan and Pakistan numbered fewer than 500 by early 2011, al-Zawahiri and other top leaders remained elusive.

The War on Terror pulled many different leaders onto the world stage. Jihadists such as Osama bin Laden and Abu Musab al-Zarqawi became the faces of 21st-century terrorism. George W. Bush and Tony Blair, as leaders of the Western world, set a contro-versial course for the pursuit of justice and the installation of new governments in Afghanistan and Iraq. And out of the chaos of war rose such figures as Hamid Karzai and Nouri al-Maliki, who aimed to lead the reconstruction efforts in their respective homelands. As the War on Terror continued into 2011 and beyond, the world waited to see which major players would emerge next.

As secretary of state, Hillary Clinton (left) pressured Pakistan to increase its pursuit of al Qaeda and Taliban militants.

A LADY OF FIRSTS

Hillary Rodham Clinton broke new ground for women in U.S. politics. During her husband Bill Clinton's 1992 presidential campaign, she showed herself to be his valuable and intelligent counterpart. As president, Bill named her to head the Task Force on National Health Reform, and in 2000, Hillary was elected to the U.S. Senate, becoming the first wife of a former president to win a national office. Clinton narrowly lost the 2008 Democratic presidential nomination to Barack Obama, but a year later, she joined his administration as secretary of state.

ENDNOTES

coalition — an alliance of individuals or groups who join together for a common cause

colonialism — the control or governing influence of one (usually powerful) nation over another nation or territory

diplomacy — non-hostile negotiations or interactions carried out between countries working toward alliances, treaties, or agreements

ideology — the system of ideas, theories, and philosophies of a group of people

insurgents — people who fight or otherwise actively participate in a revolt or uprising against a government or ruling force

intelligence — information concerning political or military matters, including potential acts by an enemy or possible enemy

jihad — a holy war waged by Muslims as a religious duty against people who do not believe in Islam

madrasas — religious schools used for teaching Islamic theology and religious law

martyrdom — the act of sacrificing something or dying for a religion or beliefs; in the world of Islam, the word "shahid" is used for Muslims who die while fulfilling religious commandments or waging war in the name of Islam

militants — people who use aggression or combat in support of a cause

mujahideen — a military force of Muslim guerrilla fighters; the word is Arabic for "holy warriors" and refers in particular to fighters during Afghanistan's resistance to Soviet occupation from 1979 to 1989

Muslim Brotherhood — a fundamentalist Islamic group founded in 1928 by Egyptian teacher Hasan al-Banna, dedicated to uniting Muslims and creating a society and government ruled by Islamic law

North Atlantic Treaty Organization (NATO) — an alliance of 28 countries in North America and Europe that provides political or military support to protect its member countries

nuclear nonproliferation — prevention of the production or spread of nuclear weapons, especially to countries that did not previously possess them

Pentagon — a huge, five-sided building near Washington, D.C., that is the headquarters of the U.S. Department of Defense

propaganda — information, ideas, or rumors that are methodically spread in order to help or harm a person, group, or movement

secular — being void of religious ties or affiliations

Shiites — members of a sect, or group, of Muslims who believe the prophet Muhammad designated his son-in-law, Ali ibn Abi Talib, as his successor; Shiites (or Shia) make up about 20 percent of Muslims worldwide

Sunni — a sect, or group, of Muslims who proclaimed Abu Bakr, a prominent disciple of the prophet Muhammad, as Muhammad's successor; Sunnis make up about 80 percent of Muslims worldwide

United Nations (UN) — an organization with representatives from 192 nations that deals with international law, human rights, and economic progress, and aims to maintain peace between nations through communication

Wahhabi — describing the beliefs of Muhammad ibn Abd al-Wahhab, an Islamic cleric who opposed all practices not sanctioned by the Qur'an (or Koran); Wahhabism, also called Salafism, was founded in the 18th century and is the most conservative form of Islam

weapons of mass destruction (WMD) — weapons such as nuclear bombs and chemicals or gases that are capable of killing large numbers of people or destroying huge areas

Cole, David. *Justice at War: The Men and Ideas That Shaped America's War on Terror.* New York: New York Review Books, 2008.

Gordon, Philip H., and Jeremy Shapiro. *Allies at War: America, Europe, and the Crisis over Iraq.* New York: McGraw-Hill, Inc., 2004.

Kepel, Gilles, and Jean-Pierre Milelli, eds. Translated by Pascale Ghazaleh. *Al Qaeda in Its Own Words.* Cambridge, Mass.: Belknap Press of Harvard University Press, 2008.

Khosrokhavar, Farhad. *Inside Jihadism: Understanding Jihadi Movements Worldwide.* Boulder, Colo.: Paradigm Publishers, 2009.

SELECTED BIBLIOGRAPHY

National Commission on Terrorist Attacks Upon the United States. *The 9/11 Commission Report: Final Report of the National Commission on Terrorist Attacks upon the United States.* New York: W. W. Norton, 2004.

Post, Jerrold M. *The Mind of the Terrorist: The Psychology of Terrorism from the IRA to al Qaeda.* New York: Palgrave Macmillan, 2007.

Riedel, Bruce. *The Search for al Qaeda: Its Leadership, Ideology, and Future.* Washington, D.C.: Brookings Institution Press, 2008.

Shultz, Richard H., and Andrea J. Dew. *Insurgents, Terrorists, and Militias: The Warriors of Contemporary Combat.* New York: Columbia University Press, 2006.